Notes on Old Edinburgh

Notes on Old Edinburgh

Victorian Travelogue Series
(Annotated)

Isabella Lucy Bird

Cedar Lake Classics

Copyright © 2023 by Cedar Lake Classics

This is a proofread and newly designed edition of a public domain work.

CONTENTS

PREFATORY NOTE BY THE REV. DR. HANNA   vii

Chapter 1   1

Chapter 2   7

Chapter 3   18

Chapter 4   29

FOOTNOTES   37
ABOUT ISABELLA LUCY BIRD   39
BOOKS BY ISABELLA LUCY BIRD   43

PREFATORY NOTE BY THE REV. DR. HANNA

Was ever a more vivid picture of more revolting scenes offered to the reader's eye than that which the following pages present? If any doubt creep into his mind as to the accuracy of its details, he has but to read the reports of Dr. Littlejohn and Dr. Alexander Wood, in which everything here stated, not vouched for by the writer herself, is authenticated. Can nothing be done, shall nothing be done, to wipe out such foul blots from the face of our fair city? One effort among others is being made in this direction by the Association recently organized for improving the condition of the poor. It is in the hope of winning for this Association the support of all the humane among us that these "Notes" are published. It would be a happy, and not surely hopeless issue, if, by the combined and concentrated endeavours of all interested in the welfare of the poor, such a change were effected that, fifty years hence, it were doubted or denied that ever such a state of things existed as is here so graphically portrayed.

W. H.
6, Castle Terrace,
Jan. 20, 1869.

Chapter 1

It has been my fortune to see the worst slums of the Thames district of London, of Birmingham, and other English and foreign cities, the "water-side" of Quebec, and the Five Points and mud huts of New York, and a short time ago a motive stronger than curiosity induced me to explore some of the worst parts of Edinburgh--not the very worst, however. Honest men can have no desire to blink facts, and no apology is necessary for stating the plain truth, as it appears to me, that there are strata of misery and moral degradation under the shadow of St. Giles's crown and within sight of Knox's house, more concentrated and unbroken than are to be met with elsewhere, even in a huge city which, by reason of a district often supposed to have no match for vice and abjectness, is continually held up to public reprobation. The Rev. R. Maguire, rector of St. James's, Clerkenwell, accompanied me through a portion only of the district visited, and he expressed his opinion then, and since more formally in print, that more dirt, degradation, overcrowding, and consequent shamelessness and unutterable wretchedness, exist in Edinburgh than in any town of twice its size, or in any area of similar extent to the one explored, taken from the worst part of London. With this opinion my own convictions cordially concur. We have plenty of awful guilt-centres in London--as, for instance, the alleys leading out of Liquorpond Street and the New Cut, but even the worst are broken in upon by healthy neighbourhoods. Here there is a loathsome infectious sore, occupying a larger area than anywhere else--a district given up in great measure to moral degradation, which extends from the Lawnmarket to Holyrood, from Holyrood along the parallel streets of the Cowgate, the Grassmarket, and the West Port, including most of the adjacent wynds and closes, and only terminating with Cowfeeder Row.

My object was to compare a certain section of Edinburgh, both by day and night, with a similar area in the city before alluded to. In company with two philanthropic gentlemen, who did not hesitate to expose these social plague-spots, and guided in one mysterious locality by one of the lieutenants of police, I explored at various times several closes in the High Street, Cowgate, and West Port, going by "house-row." In all cases the people were civil and willing to admit us, and few allowed us to depart without expressing a hope that some good would come out of the efforts proposed to be made for them. In many houses only the children were at home, but they answered our questions with such quick comprehension and painfully precocious intelligence that we were not left in doubt as to the circumstances of their parents.

It was a dry, warm morning. No rain had fallen for some weeks. There was a rumour of cholera on the Rhine, and under its salutary influence various sanitary precautions, such as lime-washing closes and stairs, had been recently resorted to. The district might have looked cheerful had cheerfulness been possible, so great was the contrast between its aspect now and its look on a wet, murky, autumn day. The appearance of the lower part of the High Street was as little pleasant as usual. Knots of men who never seem to "move on" stared at the passers-by on the South Bridge, bold girls lounged about and chaffed the soldiers, care-worn women, and little girls hardly less careworn, stood round the well with their pails--some of the last, we learned, having stood there for two and three hours. There were dirty little children as usual rolling in the gutter or sitting stolidly on the kerb-stone; as usual, haggard, wrinkled, vicious faces were looking out of the dusty windows above, and an air of joylessness, weariness, and struggle hung over all. Truly has this street been named the Via Dolorosa.

The above-named well, close by John Knox's house, is a sign of one of the standing grievances of this district of Edinburgh. It is the "water supply" of the large population living in those many-storeyed houses which give the immediate neighbourhood its picturesqueness. If it could tell the tale of one day, we should have plenty of the sensational element, but it would be the true tragedy of the real, suffering, everyday life of the poor. From six in the morning till nearly midnight, it is the centre of a throng, feminine mainly, but often essentially unwomanly in its language and manners. As a horde of thirsty pilgrims struggles for the first draught of the water of the bright oasis of the desert, so this crowd often struggles for the first turn at the tap. In its more usual condition, it is sad rather than belligerent, feeble in its scuffling, loud-voiced in its abuse. Here the weakest go to the wall. Here children carrying buckets nearly as big as themselves are sometimes known to wait from one to five hours for the water which is to wash the faces, cook the food, and quench the thirst of the family for the day. Here they wait, losing time and gaining a precocious familiarity with evil from the profanity and depravity of the talk and chaffing around them. To this well the aged widow, who struggles hard to keep up appearances, with her white mutch and neatly-pinned black shawl, totters with her pail down her dark stair of 150 steps, up the steep close, and down the street, waiting with the patience born of necessity in the heat, or rain, or snow, as the case may be, till the younger and stronger have got their "turn," and then stumbles with failing breath up her stair, the water, which is precious as that of the well of Bethlehem, spilling as she goes. At what a cost does she buy the whiteness of her mutch! Hither comes the young, weary-looking mother, having locked up her young family in her eyrie. Heavily burdened with care she looks. We may trust she forgets the perils of fire and window at home; she scuffles feebly; street brawling is a new and uncongenial thing to her, and she usually ends by losing the best part of the morning. She is slowly dropping out of her cleanly habits. Can we wonder? She thinks twice at least about scrubbing the floor, and it isn't much use to wash her children's clothes when they have no place to play in but the gutter. Here also come the small children with jugs, and hang about for a frolic, learning to curse and swear and imitate the vices of their elders, if they have not learned them before.

It is a pitiful sight in the street, but followed to the homes this lack of water helps to degrade, pity for the sufferers mingles with indignant surprise that proprietors of the best paying property to be found (for so the closes are) have not been compelled ere this to have at least a pipe and tap in every close. Outside the great Reformer's house is the well of pure water, difficult of access for most, nearly inaccessible at times to the feeble, the diffident, and the old. Under the same house is the whisky-shop, easy enough to reach, and the whisky all too easy to procure--only the laying down a few pence, and the fluid which makes life brighter for an hour is at the lips without waiting or scuffling. How can our sad and sorely-tempted ones escape the snare? Limited water and unlimited whisky, crowded dens and unwholesome air; we need nothing more to make a city full of drunkards.

We followed this water grievance into thirty-seven houses that day, and there was scarcely one in which it was not enlarged upon. Did our eyes wander round a room ever so stealthily, its occupier was ready to forestall the glance by saying, "Ah, sirs, it's the dirt ye're looking at, but how's puir folk like us to be clean as has to haul every drop of water from that well?" Did we shrink ever so slightly from a child whose head and clothing were one mass of dirt, the movement was perceived, and the want of water, the distance from the well, and the long long stair, were the apologies offered.

I merely give one instance, which might be multiplied almost indefinitely, of the distress arising from this comparatively little thought-of cause. In a wretched den on the seventh storey, none the brighter or lighter for being nearer the skies, for it had no direct light, a family, consisting of father, mother, and child of three years old, were fighting a hard battle for life. On the floor, on a straw bed, the husband had been "down with fever" for six weeks. He was wandering and murmuring incessantly, "Drink! drink!" clutching all the time at a tin pitcher by his side which contained water. He was too weak to lift it, and his wife, who expected shortly to become a mother, was helping him to it every three or four minutes. The bairn was crippled and mentally deficient, and kept crawling into the ashes, so that between it and her husband the poor woman had not a moment's rest. On a line across the room a half-washed sheet was hanging, steaming as it dried. The atmosphere in the room was poisonous. The woman said, "Ah, you are feeling the smell. Sometimes I think he'd get better if we could have things clean about us. He's got bed-sores, and you see they run a good deal, and I'm such a weak body, I can't haul water enough to wash it out of the sheets. He drinks nearly all I bring--quarts a day. He was always so fond of the water, he never tasted the whisky in his life. He's been a good husband to me; and since we've come here I can't get the water to keep him clean." In answer to inquiry, she said she had waited half an hour at the well the night before, and in coming up the long dark stair a drunk man had pushed against her and upset the whole pailful. On our expressing some sympathy, she burst into tears, sobbing out, "Oh, God only knows what it is to slave after the water--it's killing me and him too, and in the glen we came from the bonnie burn ran by the door." In that moment, some cruel memory contrasted that foul steaming sheet, whose poisonous fumes nearly overcame the strong, with the linen washed on the grass by the burn, over which the birch and harebell trembled, and bleached afterwards by the sun to the whiteness of snow. They were evicted crofters from Perthshire, and misfortune, not drink or vice, had brought them so low. Our sanitary reforms are too late for them, for both went shortly afterwards to the land where "they shall thirst no more."

Travellers have often enlarged upon the hardships suffered by the fellaheen of Egypt in carrying water for irrigating purposes. It is from the free, pure Nile they draw it at will, and over the pure alluvial soil they carry it. But this water grievance, which exists not only in the Canongate and High Street, but in the Cowgate, the Grassmarket, the West Port, and elsewhere, involves female slavery in Edinburgh of the most grinding description, and consequences from which the moralist and the philanthropist may well shrink. This want of water involves not alone a slavery which in many cases knows no Sabbath, and dirt which is a help to degradation, but an absence of all arrangements for decency. Looking at this subject from a stranger's stand-point, it seems perfectly credible that the lack of all proper water supply in these crowded districts, the impossibility which it creates of preserving physical self-respect, and the evil influence on the young of the "wait" at the wells, is one among the many causes of the lapsing of the masses in Edinburgh. The subject of the water supply is beset with difficulties, but there is a possibility of grappling with and overcoming them. The matter is more closely connected with moral reform than we might think at first sight. In England we have a proverb, "Cleanliness is next to godliness," and without indorsing it fully, we may agree that physically filthy habits and moral impurity, among the poor at least, are intimately associated. It is impossible for these people to be clean in their dwellings, clothes, or persons under present circumstances. It is inevitable that infectious diseases of the most fatal kind must be generated and diffused. It is certain that the spirit of murmuring against God is fostered by this lack of an element which these female water-carriers suppose should be free to them as light and air. The evil is becoming worse and worse as a larger and larger population crowds into these subdivided dwellings, there, perforce almost, to fall into habits lower than those of the beasts. It is well known that drunkenness, disease, and degradation are the results of a deficient water supply. It is more difficult to estimate statistically the broken health and hearts of the female water-carriers. There is an economy of water and a most prodigal expenditure of human suffering.

Chapter 2

In the Old Town, where the population of a village or a fashionable square is constantly crammed into the six or seven storeys of one house, room-to-room visitation, for it is nothing else, affords a visitor in one morning a glimpse of a state of things without a parallel. In no other city could tenements be found without gas, without water-pipes, water-closet, or sink, or temporary receptacle for ashes, and entered only by one long dark stone stair, which return such enormous profits to their owners as from 45 to 60 per cent. Scarcely elsewhere does one roof cover a population of 290, 248, 240 persons, living in dens, honeycombed out of larger rooms, without ventilation, without privacy, and often without direct light. In no other city is the respectable mechanic compelled, for want of house accommodation of a proper kind, to bring up his family in a tenement which deserves indictment as a nuisance, or to pay £5, £6, or £8 a year for a den swarming with vermin, with only a wooden partition to keep off the sights and admit all the sounds of haunts of the most degraded vice. In Edinburgh, which, in more respects than one, is set on a hill and cannot be hid, there are 13,209 families, comprising not only the vicious and abject, but large numbers of the poorer labouring class, living in houses of but one room, and of these single rooms, 1530 are inhabited by from six to fifteen persons! Further, by the last census, 120 of these shelters, for they are not houses, were reported as without windows, and 900 were cellars, nearly all of them dark, and many damp. These figures give the astounding result that the families living in one room, and often herding together in closer proximity than animals would endure, comprehend 66,000 persons, or considerably more than one-third of the population of Edinburgh! [1]

The notes which follow are merely a commentary upon the above facts. My room-to-room visitation on a single day included thirty-seven families residing in a close south of the High Street and ten families in a close south of the Cowgate. I do not give the names of either, in deference to the feelings of respectable persons who are compelled by various causes to reside in them.

The entrance of the close which we selected is long and narrow, and so low as to compel a man of average height to stoop. It is paved with round stones, and from the slime in which they were embedded, and from a grating on one side almost choked up with fish heads and insides, and other offal, a pungent and disgusting effluvium was emitted. The width of this close is four feet at the bottom, but the projecting storeys of the upper houses leave only a narrow strip of quiet sky to give light below. A gutter ran along one side of the close against the wall, and this, though so early in the day, was in a state of loathsomeness not to be described. Very ragged children, infinitely more ragged and dirty than those which offend our eyes in the open street, were sitting on the edge of this gutter, sitting as if they meant to sit there all day; not playing, not even quarrelling, just stupefying. Foul air, little light, and bad food had already done their work on most of them. Blear eyes, sore faces, and sore feet were almost universal. Their matted hair and filthy rags were full of vermin. Their faces were thin, pinched, and precocious. Many of them had been locked out in the morning when their mothers went to their hawking, washing, and other occupations, and might be locked out till midnight, or later, as we found on the following night. There they sat, letting the slow, vile stream in the gutter run over their feet, and there they were sitting three hours later. They were from three to ten years old. It is all the same if the rain or snow is falling, except that they leave the gutters to huddle together in the foul shelter of the stair-foot. Some of these will die, many will be educated into the hardened criminality of the often-imprisoned street boy, many will slide naturally into a life of shame, and a fortunate few will be sentenced to reformatories, from whence they come out decent members of society at the rate of 70 per cent. "God help them!" exclaimed a mother, so drunk that her own babe seemed in peril in her arms. Ay, God help them! But our Father which is in heaven charges the responsibility of their destiny on the respectable men and women of Edinburgh.

We entered the first room by descending two steps. It seemed to be an old coal-cellar, with an earthen floor, shining in many places from damp, and from a greenish ooze which drained through the wall from a noxious collection of garbage outside, upon which a small window could have looked had it not been filled up with brown paper and rags. There was no grate, but a small fire smouldered on the floor, surrounded by heaps of ashes. The roof was unceiled, the walls were rough and broken, the only light came in from the open door, which let in unwholesome smells and sounds. No cow or horse could thrive in such a hole. It was abominable. It measured eleven feet by six feet, and the rent was 10d. per week, paid in advance. It was nearly dark at noon, even with the door open; but as my eyes became accustomed to the dimness, I saw that the plenishings consisted of an old bed, a barrel with a flagstone on the top of it for a table, a three-legged stool, and an iron pot. A very ragged girl, sorely afflicted with ophthalmia, stood among the ashes doing nothing. She had never been inside a school or church. She did not know how to do anything, but "did for her father and brother." On a heap of straw, partly covered with sacking, which was the bed in which father, son, and daughter slept, the brother, ill with rheumatism and sore legs, was lying moaning from under a heap of filthy rags. He had been a baker "over in the New Town," but seemed not very likely to recover. It looked as if the sick man had crept into his dark, damp lair, just to die of hopelessness. The father was past work, but "sometimes got an odd job to do." The sick man had supported the three. It was hard to be godly, impossible to be cleanly, impossible to be healthy in such circumstances.

The next room was entered by a low, dark, impeded passage about twelve feet long, too filthy to be traversed without a light. At the extremity of this was a dark winding stair which led up to four superincumbent storeys of crowded subdivided rooms; and beyond this, to the right, a pitch-dark passage with a "room" on either side. It was not possible to believe that the most grinding greed could extort money from human beings for the tenancy of such dens as those to which this passage led. They were lairs into which a starving dog might creep to die, but nothing more. Opening a dilapidated door, we found ourselves in a recess nearly 6 feet high, and 9 feet in length by 5 in breadth. It was not absolutely dark, yet matches aided our investigations even at noon-day. There was an earthen floor full of holes, in some of which water had collected. The walls were black and rotten, and alive with wood-lice. There was no grate. The rent paid for this evil den, which was only ventilated by the chimney, is 1s. per week, or £2, 12s. annually! The occupier was a mason's labourer, with a wife and three children. He had come to Edinburgh in search of work, and could not afford a "higher rent." The wife said that her husband took the "wee drap." So would the President of the Temperance League himself if he were hidden away in such a hole. The contents of this lair on our first visit were a great heap of ashes and other refuse in one corner, some damp musty straw in another, a broken box in the third, with a battered tin pannikin upon it, and nothing else of any kind, saving two small children, nearly nude, covered with running sores, and pitiable from some eye disease. Their hair was not long, but felted into wisps, and alive with vermin. When we went in they were sitting among the ashes of an extinct fire, and blinked at the light from our matches. Here a neighbour said they sat all day, unless their mother was merciful enough to turn them into the gutter. We were there at eleven the following night, and found the mother, a decent, tidy body, at "hame." There was a small fire then, but no other light. She complained of little besides the darkness of the house, and said, in a tone of dull discontent, she supposed it was "as good as such as they could expect in Edinburgh." The two children we had seen before were crouching near the embers, blinking at a light we carried, and on the musty straw in the corner a third, about ten years old, was doubled up. This child had not a particle of clothing, but was partially covered with a rag of carpet. She was ill of scrofula, and the straw she lay on seemed to be considered a luxury. Three adults (including a respectable-looking grandmother) and three children slept on that unwholesome floor, in a room, be it remembered, 9 by 5, and under 6 feet high. We allow each convict 500 cubic feet of air in his cell. "We consider him as one to be washed, clothed, covered, ventilated; secularly, technically, and religiously taught, regularly exercised, and profitably employed. We do not fling him into a dark hole, even when he misbehaves himself, and we do not leave him there for years to fester in filth."--Daily Telegraph, April 3, 1868. This reads like a bitter satire on what we do to such families as these. On the other side of the dark passage there was a room somewhat larger, for which a rent of 1s. 6d. per week was obtained. This had no window or outer wall, and its sole ventilation was by means of a hole in the door.

These two lairs were the worst specimens of basement-storey rooms in that close, but the rest were not much better, and their occupiers (all Scotch) were equally poor. Medical men, with that noble spirit of philanthropy which adorns the profession in Edinburgh, know these dens, and the city and parochial missionaries, wearied and discouraged, still speak to the dwellers in them of One who is mighty to save. But they have long cried to the rich, to the men and women of leisure, to the Churches, "Come over and help us." They ask people to throw aside their theories, to cease wrangling over the cause, and try a rational cure; to give the poor not what the rich and benevolent like, but what the poor know they need--and that is, houses to dwell in, not dens to rot and perish in, morally and physically. Blissful ignorance of the abyss of preventible misery which exists in Edinburgh is impossible now. There are many divers at work, and not one returns to the surface without bringing some cumulative proof of the wreck and ruin below. No person, stranger or citizen, who believes the facts can shirk an individual responsibility concerning them. If sanitary reforms and city improvement schemes come too late to save a lapsed generation of adults, kindly contact with the rich, discriminating charity, houses in which cleanliness and decency are possible, may redeem the children. It was with a little hope for them, at least, that we turned from the close that day; a little hope, I say, for the dawn of the day which is to save them has not yet appeared. After the many diseased dismal infants crouching in their dark dens on the sunny day, the children of the gutters seemed almost happy, for they could see above the lofty houses a blue strip of sky, beyond which, they might have heard, dwells their Father. But hideous blasphemies all around came forth from infant lips, and of that stinted, joyless, loveless, misused childhood, if left to itself, an impure, unholy manhood and womanhood can be the only end. Did the Master declare of these, and the legion of these, "of such is the kingdom of heaven?" What then?

Leaving these basement dens we entered another close, whose lofty houses, with overhanging wooden fronts, give a certain amount of picturesqueness, while they exclude light to such a degree that it is never much more than twilight below, even on a sunny day. It is said that these projecting fronts were built of wood from Boroughmuir, presented by a devout King wherewith to provide oratories for the inhabitants of this close--so that every one of them might be in circumstances to obey the command, "But thou, when thou prayest, enter into thy closet, and when thou hast shut thy door, pray to thy Father which is in secret." If the tradition be true, it renders the use to which these oratories are now applied, and the condition of the occupants of these dwellings, more sad and revolting by contrast. Though the light in the close was little better than twilight, several women were standing outside the houses mending and patching. They said they could not see to do a stitch indoors. There were many children sitting in the gutters, very dirty, ragged, and sore-eyed. These, the women said, were the children of parents too poor to provide them with clothes fit to go into the street. Out of sixty-two children of families visited in this close, twenty only are reported as attending school. This statement, probably, is above the real number, as among the thirty-two families visited by myself, there was only one child reported as attending school. So these children, who don't go to school, and are too ragged to be sent to disport themselves in the street, spend their time between their crowded dens upstairs and the narrow, filthy close--for filthy it was, even at midday, although it was paved, and the scavengers had not finished their work more than five hours before. These children have never known cleanliness or decency. The happiness which comes from chasing butterflies, rooting up pig-nuts, and making daisy wreaths, has never come their way; or even the less Arcadian jollities of trundling hoops, playing at marbles, and making dirt-pies, in which city children delight themselves elsewhere. But these are "cribbed, cabined, and confined" by the high black walls, and, as a mother said, "they are learning the devil's lessons well." It is no exaggeration to add that many of them are as absolutely ignorant of love as they are of cleanliness, decency, and happiness. Locked out into the cold or wet, scantily clad, meanly fed, kicked about in the morning, kicked about at night, cursed instead of kissed, utterly neglected in body and soul, they grow up attaching no meaning whatever to the words love and home. The wynds and closes are swarming with them, the ragged and industrial schools, when they get hold of them, are fain to withdraw them by night as well as by day from what in mockery are called their homes, if they are to do anything with them. As long as these are suffered to be born and reared in dens, so long must we build prisons, reformatories, and Magdalene asylums to teach them, at enormous cost, the decencies they have never known. In going through this close, and several of the poorer districts, I have become aware that a very large number of the parents of these forlorn infants are literally and consciously "lapsed." By their willing and frequently regretful admission they were "well-doing before they came to Edinburgh," or they were once better off in Edinburgh, and "have come down in the world;" they were Church members, and had the friendly recognition of ministers and elders; they "paid their way," etc. etc. From one and all of these they have "lapsed," some by drink, others by misfortune; and this was the case with a large proportion of the inhabitants of this "land," in whose deep wretchedness and degradation they are wallowing, and on whose threshold the reader is being detained. But be it solemnly remembered, the children who "are learning the devil's lessons" in the gutter start not from the platform of well-doing from which many of the parents fell, but from the platform of vice, intemperance, godlessness, recklessness, and filth to which the parents have fallen.

Of such as these, one who claims a hearing for their woes and their helplessness (Dr. Guthrie), writes--"I know the lapsed and wretched classes well. I believe if I was as poor as they I should be as deceitful. Circumstances make people what they are much more than many suppose. There is not a wretched child in this town but if my children had been born and bred up in its unhappy circumstances they might have been as bad."

The smell of this close was intolerable. How can it be otherwise when all the solid and liquid refuse which has been accumulating in the densely packed habitations during the day, lies in the narrow close from ten at night, in such quantities that the scavengers not unfrequently remove nearly a ton of it at seven in the morning, and the ground and the foundations of the houses are saturated with the liquid refuse and drainage? [2]

I only give a sketch of the general conformation and circumstances of the lands in this close, premising that the description--often very much darkened in tint, however--applies to a majority of the Old Town abodes which, in Edinburgh, are considered good property, and fit for the stowage of human beings, in Murdoch's Close, Hume's Close, Skinner's Close, Hyndford's Close, South Foulis' Close, Cant's Close, Blackfriars Wynd, Todrick's Wynd, Plainstone Close, Campbell's Close, Brown's Close, etc., to which citizens who take an interest in this painful subject can add various other closes on both sides of the High Street and Canongate, many stairs in the Cowgate, and various entries and closes in the Grassmarket and West Port. It is supposed that not fewer than 40,000 people live in habitations not superior to, and often much inferior to, the lands hereafter described.

The entrance to the first "land" visited was by a very long, narrow, winding stair, with steps so worn as to be unsafe. The stair was as dark by day as by night until near the top, and there was nothing to assist an unsteady walker in his ascent or descent. The wall was broken, and, as we found on striking a light, the cracks swarmed with bugs and other vermin, as, indeed, does every fissure and cranny of the dilapidated tenements above. We had not gone far before the stench which assailed us was worse than that from the worst-kept pigstye, and we found the state of the stair too disgusting for description. It is disgraceful, degrading, shameful; and who is to blame? A stranger at once supposes that it is due partly to the filthy habits of the people, and also to the crime of the landlords in not lighting the stairs. This last is a criminal act as regards cleanliness, morals, and safety, and its continuance ought not to be permitted for another month. The regulation concerning the cleaning of stairs cannot be carried out in the dark, even if the people had brooms, which most of them have not, and if they had a "spigot" in the close instead of having to haul every drop of water from a public well at some distance. There is an infinite injustice and degradation in such a mode of access and egress for frail old age, and infancy scarcely less frail, for females heavily laden with water or refuse-buckets, for young girls, and for men savagely or boisterously drunk, in many cases for a population over 200.

On each landing there was a passage branching into several smaller ones, very much like the galleries in a coal-pit, burrowing in and out among endlessly subdivided rooms, measuring from 18 feet by 10 feet to 9 feet by 5 feet, separated by skeleton partitions filled up with plaster, through which any man can put his foot. In this case the long passage was outside the congeries of habitations, and was lighted on two floors by the windows of the recesses before alluded to as having been the oratories of past generations. They had served the greed of late proprietors, for a great number of the rooms partitioned off from the passage were dimly lighted by windows looking upon it. Ventilated they could not be, for the smell in this passage was poisonous. Nothing shows more forcibly the lapsing of houses, as well as of human beings, than the fact that these recesses, once prized as places for prayer, are now highly valued for another purpose, being receptacles during the day for multitudes of battered pails, containing the ashes and refuse hourly accumulating in the rooms. Those persons consider themselves well off who have any such public recesses or corners which can be used for this purpose. In general, in these tenements, the inhabitants are compelled to keep the pail and "backet," containing the unwholesome accumulations of the day, under the bed, if there be one, and, failing that, in any corner, from seven in the morning till ten at night. In large young families, and in sickness and old age, the result may be imagined, when these accumulations of refuse of all descriptions are shut up in rooms without ventilation, along with the steam of half-washed clothes, in air contaminated by the respiration of several persons. In this land the average size of the rooms is 12 feet by 7 feet. If, on the one hand, drink brings people into these abodes, on the other, the foul, vile, depressing air, joined to the want of light and water, drives them in thousands to the dram-shop. There was scarcely a woman whose face did not testify, by its depression, yellowness, and emaciation, to the air she is compelled to breathe by day and night. Besides that the absence of temporary receptacles for refuse is utterly disgusting and injurious to health, it inflicts sore toil on the women, who are more than sufficiently burdened with drawing water from the public wells. It is not a small thing for the mother of a family, or a frail old wife, to come down the dark filthy stair late at night with the "ashbacket," even if there be a window half-way down from which she may discharge the contents on the pavement below.

All along the passages there were thin partitions stuffed with rags, where the plaster had fallen out, or had been kicked through in some drunken frenzy--doors so broken all round that privacy even from the gaze of passing strangers is impossible--a roof, in part, nothing better than old boards, strengthened with pieces of iron and tin, which, like everything else here, had "seen better days"--floors rotten--so rotten as to require big stones to fill up holes larger than a man's head--windows with hardly any glass left in them--wind and rain coming in in many places--the whole pile apparently little more than just holding together by sheer force of habit, utterly unfit for human habitation as it is--a disgrace which public opinion ought to be strong enough to condemn. But it is one of a legion of similar disgraces; it is a lucrative sin, a paying shame; in politer language, it is "a good investment!" Ay, a good investment! For these cabins, which, by a pernicious fiction, are called "houses," are rack-rented at from £2, 10s. to £5 each, and pay the fortunate proprietors from 40 to 60 per cent. Here are "vested interests" with a vengeance!

Chapter 3

This rickety "land" is not by any means in one of the worst closes in Edinburgh. It is not a haunt of the criminal classes. Vice and virtue live side by side, though the virtuous are in a miserable minority, and their children are in grievous peril of vice. I was given to understand, by those well acquainted with the city, that it was a good representative specimen of an average "land" in a High Street close. On that and another occasion we visited thirty-two families, going by room-row. I propose to give the circumstances of a few families, taken after this fashion. All the rooms were in themselves wretched, few more than half-lighted, scarcely any capable of ventilation, some on the second-floor requiring candles at mid-day, floors and partitions in a shameful condition, the former in many instances containing holes as big as a man's head, stuffed with stones; the latter very thin and dilapidated, mended with rags, bits of canvas, tin, and paper. The doors were usually made of odds and ends of old boards, so rudely put together that in some rooms the people had nailed canvas over them to prevent strangers from looking in. The windows were nearly all bad, and patched with brown paper; no gas or water. The landlord had never repaired anything within the memory of the "oldest inhabitant." Among all the people visited the complaints were the same--rapacious landlords charging from £2, 10s. to £5; no repairs executed; borrowed light, involving an addition to the rent in the shape of 1s. per week for candles; want of privacy; distance of water supply; dark stairs; increasing subdivision of rooms, involving, in some cases, the intense hardship of a right of way through the outer room. It is due to all these people to say, that while they readily answered all our questions, they never begged of us, or even hinted that charity would be acceptable. It is due to some of them also to say, that their attempts to keep their wretched dwellings clean were most praiseworthy.

First room, 11 feet by 5 feet. A box-bed took up a third of it. No grate; fire burning on a stone. The furniture consisted of the bed, a table with three legs, and a "creepie." The room had direct light from a small patched window, which was not made to open. The walls were broken, and almost to pieces. There was a hole in the floor filled up with a large stone. The occupier, a mason's labourer, was out seeking work, and his wife was at the well. These two adults and five children between three and fourteen years old slept on the floor, the eldest child said. "But don't your father and mother sleep on the bed?" we asked. "No, they can't for the bugs; we just lies on the floor, all of a heap." "In your clothes?" "No; we takes them off." "Do you put anything on?" "No; we's just naked." Truly, they had nothing to put on if they did succeed in getting out of the wonderful aggregation of rags which hung on to them. For there were no blankets, or any covering but an old piece of carpet. The rent was £3, 10s. a year. The girl who made this frank revelation was extremely pretty and intelligent. Her young brother and sisters were beautiful, but absolutely filthy; their arms and legs were covered with sores, and their matted hair alive with vermin. The father was the only one of the family who could read. The girl said that her father's leg had gone through the floor up to the knee, and then they put the stone in the hole. From this account it appears that, after deducting the space occupied by the bed, seven individuals huddle together all of a heap in an area 6 feet by 5 feet. The room was damp and draughty.

The next room was 18 feet by 10 feet; shamefully out of repair, the wooden partition falling to pieces. Some of the holes in it were carefully patched with paper, but the neighbours constantly tear this off to look in. One of the so-called panels of the door had been kicked in by a drunken man; the landlord would not repair it, so the occupant had nailed a piece of canvas over it. The window-glass was mostly gone, and though the window had originally been made to open, the sash was too rotten to be touched. The floor was in holes in several places. The rain came in along one wall. The rent is £4. The family consisted of an elderly father and mother, and two sons, plumbers. The father and eldest son had been out of work for some time, and the youngest was only getting better from a fever. They were very reticent about their circumstances, but we gathered that two daughters in service were supporting them. Both father and mother were rheumatic from the damp of the house, they said. There were two beds, but they "can't sleep on either,--alive with bugs from the walls," so take refuge on the floor. The woman pulled aside a patch of canvas, and showed the wall swarming with these pests. They had taken every means of destroying them, but in vain. The room was scrupulously clean. The next measured 11 feet by 5, and 6 feet at the highest part. A single pane of glass in a corner under the roof let in as much light as made objects discernible. The plenishings consisted of a filthy straw bed, a bit of carpet, and an iron pot. The floor was almost covered with cinders, and mended in three places with stones. The room was loathsome, the smell overpowering, the look of abject and uncared-for misery sickening. The occupants were a widow, a cinder-picker, and her two children, very poor. The children were "learning the devil's lessons" in the close below. A neighbour told us that the mother often locks them into the room from five o'clock in the morning till ten or eleven at night. The rent is £2, 12s.

The next room was a house of ill-fame, with seven occupants, very disorderly, and much complained of by the neighbours on each side, who were separated from it only by a wretched partition.

The next room was almost dark; 11 feet by 5 feet; rent, 1s. per week. Its sole occupant was a frightful-looking hag, apparently more than seventy years old, a mass of rags and filth, with an uncovered hoary head, whose long locks were tangled with neglect and dirt. She was sleeping off the effects of a drunken debauch on some old straw, but woke up sufficiently to mutter a curse, and glower upon us a moment with her bloodshot eyes. She had received the parish allowance the day before, and this was the result--a whisky-bottle, without a cork, but not quite empty, was lying beside her. There was no other sign of human habitation, and in the wretched object lying on the straw we could hardly recognise humanity.

Our next visit was of a different kind. Reaching the topmost floor, we came upon a passage, very dilapidated, but lighted by a large projecting window. A very respectable artisan was lime-washing the passage, the roof, and the top of the stair. He said it was the best he could do, and he did it once a fortnight. He had two rooms, only one of which had direct light. They were like all the rest, in utter disrepair. He leant against the outer partition, which swerved considerably from the perpendicular as he did so, and said, "The weight of two men would bring it down." He came to a situation in Edinburgh, has good wages, and could meet with nothing better than this at the term. The rent is £9 a year. He gave a revolting account of the immorality of the stair. He had three young children, he said; if he couldn't get into a decent neighbourhood he'd rather see them in their graves than grow up there. "What can I hope for my bairns," he added, "when they can't get a breath of fresh air without seeing such as yon?" Looking out, we saw in a window, not a pistol-shot off, three debased women, sitting in the broad daylight, absolutely nude, as far as we could see of them. The worthy citizens who were with me blushed for the city called so fair, in which an honest artisan, with money in his pocket, was compelled to shelter his family where all sights and sounds were polluting, feeling, as he did, the abhorrent shame. The top of the stair was much broken, and destitute of any protection. A fall would have been into about forty feet of darkness. On our alluding to this as a great peril for the young children, the man said, with a bitter smile, "Bairns reared in such places are like lambs born among precipices--they early learn to take care of themselves." This is true, or the juvenile population of these closes would be decimated. Of the sad sights we saw that morning, that was about the saddest--the honest man and his shame, and the helplessness of his circumstances. It was enough to make even "polite indifference" put forth some redeeming effort.

First room on fifth floor, 12 by 14 feet. Rent £2, 10s. Very cold; roof out of repair, and admitting rain; the partitions much broken.

The occupiers were a very decent-looking man, seventy-six years old, by trade a shoemaker, his wife, aged seventy-three, and a dumb grandson, who was mending a shoe on the stool on which his grandfather "had sat for sixty-two years." They had parish relief. The woman had been in bed twelve months with paralysis, and suffered much from being removed. The dirt and vermin were perfectly awful. She was a miserable object; apparently she had no bed-gown, and her skeleton chest and ribs, which were exposed to view, might have served as a model for death. Both she and her husband had the speech and air of having seen better days. They had lived in this attic for twenty years, and had had typhus fever twice during the last ten. The rent had been raised £1 during the same period. They had five children, scattered in Australia and America, but letters addressed to them were returned with the notice "Not found." They seemed very poor, but made no complaint of anything but the wretched condition of the room, the cold and damp, the want of privacy, and the distance from which the old man had to bring the water up the long dark stair. The room was clean, with the exception of the bed, but the cracks in the partitions there, as everywhere else, were "alive with bugs." The old man said he was a church-member, and paid 2s. 6d. a year for a seat at a U.P. church. This was their own account of themselves, and the general appearance of things bore it out. Such are the cases in which much may be done, by systematic visitation, in the way of arresting a downward course. These people are now in the Poor-house, the dram-shop having proved too much for the old man.

Next room, 8 feet by 9 feet. A most wretched place, only fit to be pulled down; borrowed light. A joiner, in very bad health, and consequently out of work for two years, with his wife and four children, and a daughter by a former marriage, with an illegitimate child, were the occupants. The wife and grown-up daughter earn 7s. 6d. per week by washing. The rent is £2 a year. A most miserable family, utterly gone to wreck.

Next room.--A blind labourer, very frail, with a wife, who supports the family and four children. After an illness, were ordered into the

Poor-house, then out again, and were quite broken up by it. This room was wretched in every respect--9 feet by 10 feet, very low, and rented at £2. In the next room there was a very sad case--a compositor, with a wife and two children, living in a room, requiring a candle at mid-day, 12 feet by 8 feet; roof mended with tin, letting in the rain; floor broken and mended with stones, so rotten that a walking-stick went through it in two places. The man's joints were stiff with rheumatism, caught in the damp cold of the room. Work had slackened, and after having had a good room in Carrubbers Close, they had come here. The man had had no work for a long time, and they had pledged everything, till they had only "the clothes they stood in." They had had good furniture, but it "was all gone to keep life in them." They spoke of their poverty very reluctantly, and very warmly of the kindness of the missionary. Both man and wife were steady. Her earnings supported them; but she was expecting her confinement shortly.

The next room was 14 feet by 8 feet, and the remains of a cornice held on to the outer wall. The side walls were skeleton partitions, dilapidated and swarming with bugs. There were three doors. The occupant was a fish-hawker, an Irishwoman--cheery and self-asserting, voluble as to herself and her neighbours. Had she been of smaller size and milder tongue the hardship of which she complained would have had more pathos about it; but even as it is, a more infamous injustice could scarcely be perpetrated by the proprietors of these ruinous fabrics: her room had been subdivided since she came; she continued to pay the old rent--£4. The occupants of the inner room were a man and woman, with two lodgers, apparently of most irregular habits, who came through her room with a passkey, drunk and sober, at all hours of day and night. This is one of eleven instances of passage-rooms that I have seen in Edinburgh. In the Cowgate this infamous system flourishes, and occasionally to such an extent that the outer room is the only mode of ingress and egress for three or four others. The insult and hardship this plan entails upon the virtuous, and the facilities for immorality that it affords to the vicious cannot be recited here.

Outside this woman's room there was a perfect labyrinth of passages, all dark, but on opening a door we entered a room 12 feet square, with direct light, but with rotten partitions, like all the rest, and so pervious to sound that we heard every word of a narrative of our visit which the "decent widder" before mentioned was giving to an incomer. This room was miserable. Ashes, the accumulation of days, heaped the floor round the fire. There was no other furniture than a bedstead with a straw mattress upon it, a table, and a stool; but it was the occupants, rather than the apparent poverty, who claimed our attention. A girl about eighteen, very poorly dressed, was sitting on the stool; two others, older and very much undressed, were sitting on the floor, and the three were eating, in most swinish fashion, out of a large black pot containing fish. I have shared a similar meal, in a similar primitive fashion, in an Indian wigwam in the Hudson's Bay Territory, but there the women who worshipped the Great Spirit were modest in their dress and manner, and looked human, which these "Christian" young women did not. An infant of about a month old, perfect in its beauty, and smiling in its sleep, "as though heaven lay about it," was on the bed, not dressed, but partly covered with a rug. What better could be desired for it than that the angels might take it speedily away from that shameful birth-chamber to behold its Father's face in heaven? Easier by far to trust it in death to His mercy, than in life to the zeal of the Christianity of Edinburgh. Death for these is better than life; and, in many cases, drugs and neglect soon bring it about. "Where are you from?" one of my philanthropic companions asked of the girl of eighteen, the mother. "Dundee; mother and I came here five weeks ago. I was a mill-worker." "Will the father of your child marry you?" "No, sir." "Have you got work here?" "No, sir; I can't get any." "What are you going to do, then?" "I suppose I must do as the others." She gave this answer without shame, and without effrontery. An upbringing in a Dundee "pend" had not acquainted her with shame as an attendant upon sin. Alas for the hundreds of girl-children growing up among the debasing circumstances of the crowded "lands" of our wynds and closes, without even the instincts of virtue!

The next room, though miserable in itself, was clean and well furnished, with pictures hanging upon the partitions. A mother and daughter, both widows, but earning a good living by needlework, were the occupants. They complained bitterly of the gross viciousness of the stair, and of the "awful riot" kept up all night by those newcomers. They told us that the wretched old hag who had come from Dundee had five female lodgers, with only two gowns among them all, and that they were of the poorest and most degraded class. These respectable widows, both elderly women, had lived in that room for seven years, and in the main had had quiet neighbours. They now found themselves in this close proximity to a den of vice, unable to exclude the sounds which came through the thin partition, and too terrified at night by the drinking and uproar to be able to sleep. The term was lately passed, so they were compelled to bear it.

A few sentences more will take us through the remaining rooms on the two floors we are investigating. There follow a widow, who binds shoes, with two children, sleeping in a large bed in a room 11 feet by 9 feet, with a small window, letting in air too impure to breathe; rent, £2, 12s. A widow, with a brother seventy-two years old, poor, but clean, chiefly dependent on a daughter in service. A mason's labourer, who once farmed six acres of land, now earns 12s. per week; wife with bad eyes, and health too delicate for work, having fretted herself into decline for two children who had died of the cholera; room, 12 feet by 8 feet, rented at 1s. 2d. per week. Three adults and six children in a room 12 feet by 10 feet, without direct light. Drunken labourer, earning 15s. per week--two sons in prison; two daughters living with him, with three illegitimate children; room, 14 feet by 15 feet; rent, £3, 18s. a year. Pauper widow, with one child and two unregistered lodgers. Married labourer, with two children, earning 15s. per week; three lodgers (prostitutes) in the same room, 14 feet by 12 feet; rent, £3, 18s.; borrowed light; no furniture; all drunken together. Then follow five families, all wretched; and we have completed our room-to-room visitation of two floors in an average land in an average close in the High Street.

As seen thus, in broad daylight, except for the filth, dilapidation, vermin, darkness, and poverty, combined with the suggestions of immoral conduct on the part of most of the people, there was nothing peculiarly startling to any one at all acquainted with the Old Town of Edinburgh. I have taken this particular close, for the especial reason that what is said of it and its inhabitants applies to dwellings and circumstances in which possibly 40,000 people pass their days. I have given the impression made by it upon a stranger, in preference to depicting entries in a part of the town with which I am well acquainted, and which, in many of their aspects, are far worse. There are cellar-dwellings, damp and dark, old byres with open drains still running through them, let for human beings; garrets, damp and draughty, in which a man can scarcely stand upright; and cabins, of which stairs, roofs, and walls are mainly of wood. There are rooms as small as any I have mentioned, occupied by one, two, and three families, only reached by passage-rooms as small and crowded as themselves; and in these dens the whole round of human life goes on--agonies of birth and death, miseries of sickness and sorrow, marriage jollifications, funeral revels, the cold remains of mortality lying on the same straw with the living; the miserable meal on the table, the unshrouded corpse on the floor. Are such woes as these, such absolute savage degradation, the inevitable deposit of the highest Christian civilisation? Is there, indeed, no balm in Gilead--is there no physician there? Is it the curse of God's indignation, or the curse of man's selfishness, avarice, and neglect, under which those thousands are lying? Is this the "good ground" on which the gospel seed is to spring up and bear fruit one hundredfold? Are the rich and godly to send missionaries and Bible-women among these masses, and save their own souls by giving the necessary funds? Shall they not rather go down themselves among the lost, as Christ went, and learn their needs, and find from themselves that foremost among these are decent dwellings in which it might be possible to live and die otherwise than as swine. We might then hear less of money lying at two per cent. in the banks, or lost in insolvent railroads, and more of 8, 10, and 12 per cent. as a certain return. Talk of the risk of house property! Is it greater than the risks people have contentedly run for years in railroads, mines, and cotton? Possibly every £100 spent on improving the dwellings of the poor might do something towards accumulating a treasure in the heavens that faileth not, where no thief approacheth, or moth corrupteth.

The walls of the Old Town houses are generally strong. Such a "land" as that which I have described, gutted from cellar to roof, and supplied with water, gas, and a temporary receptacle for rubbish, would make a good substantial house at a comparatively small cost, with a certain return of from 8 to 10 per cent. The removal of the subdividing partitions, new floors, doors, and windows would be a necessity. The good result of such an undertaking in every close and wynd would not be only the placing of sixteen or eighteen families in a position in which, if they were so minded, they could be moral and religious, but the insertion of a wedge into this hardened stratum of viciousness and poverty. The bad could not be so bad in close proximity to the virtuous. The filthy would aspire to be something better. The landlords, the hardest class of all to deal with, would be compelled, by competition and opinion, to amend their property and their ways. Decent houses in St. Bernard's or St. Leonard's have no more influence over the manners and morals of Hume's Close or Todrick's Wynd than decent houses in Moray Place or Chester Street; but decent lands put down in Cant's Close or Skinner's Close, with rooms rented from £2, 10s. to £4, would do a better work of reformation around them than all the agencies which are at work.

It is only necessary to refer to the complete renovation of Warden's Close, Grassmarket, by Dr. Foulis, as a proof of what is to be done by energetic individual action. The restored fabric, as arranged for human beings, pays 14 per cent. Of course, the still greater overcrowding of other dens during the renovation of even one "land" requires to be carefully provided against.

It has been frequently stated that a third of the inhabitants of Edinburgh are not in connexion with any Christian Church. In the thirty-two families visited in ---- Close, two women were the only persons who professed to attend any place of worship. In another small close which we visited none but a Catholic family professed to attend any church. Eight years ago, in two populous stairs in another part of the town with which I was well acquainted, there was a total of nine persons attending church out of an adult population of forty. At the present time this number is reduced to one woman, who, "when she goes anywhere, goes to Lady Yester's." Of the thirty-two families before spoken of, most of the women and some of the men had formerly been church-goers. Where is this "lapsing" to end?

Chapter 4

I have given the aspect of the houses and population of a particular district by daylight, avoiding all sensational details. The "night side" of the same is well known from description--the High Street filled with a densely compacted, loitering, brawling, buying, selling, singing, cursing, quarrelsome crowd--every fifth man and woman the worse for drink so early as ten at night--a nocturnal market vigorously proceeds under difficulties--men and women puff their wares with stentorian tones and coarse wit--barrows with flaring lights, from which the poorest of the poor are buying the unwholesome refuse of the shops, stale fish, and stale vegetables--boys vending laces, nuts, whistles--women hawking tin and crockery ware, all eager, pushing, poor. Add to these, the exhibitors of penny-shows and penny cheats, the singers of low and improper songs, the vendors of popular melodies and penny narrations of crime, and an idea may be formed of the noisy traffic of the High Street. As the night goes on, the crowd becomes more drunk and criminal until the legal hour of closing the spirit-shops, when hundreds of pallid, ragged wretches are vomited forth upon the street to carry terrors into their dark, crowded homes. The majority are half-mad, and almost wholly desperate. Men and women, savage with drink, are biting, scratching, mauling each other; the air is laden with blasphemies, brutal shouts from the strong; cries from the weak; blows are dealt aimlessly; infants at midnight cry in the wet street for mothers drunk in the gutters or police cells; young girls and boys are locked out for the night by parents frantic with drink, viragos storm, policemen here and there drag an offender out of the crowd amidst the chaffing and coarse laughter of young girls bearing the outward marks of a life of degradation; mothers with infants in their arms lie helpless in the gutters, to be trundled off to the final ignominy of the police cell, wretches scarcely clothed, whom the daylight knows not, slink stealthily to some foul cellar lair,--and all this, and worse than this, from the Tron down the Canongate, and along the Cowgate, and in the Grassmarket, and in numbers of the lanes and alleys, broad and narrow, which border upon them. The district we visited by day we visited also by night, to find that at 11 P.M. the whole population of the lands previously described was astir, mostly from evil, partly from the impossibility of quiet; that small children were still out among the influences of the closes and the street, and that there was no sign that the night had come, except the darkness and the increased overcrowding of many of the rooms. The dark, narrow passages were in several places almost impassable, owing to the dead-drunk men who lay across them; the rooms were thronged and stifling, and sick and well, drunk and sober, vicious and virtuous, were all huddled together with only a pretence of separation. Whole families were sitting in the dark, or cowering round fires which only rendered the darkness visible. "A horror of great darkness" rested on all the houses. The noise was hideous. Decent people might well be afraid of going to bed. Half the inmates were under the influence of drink. Drunkards tumbled up the long dark stairs, and reeled down the dark passages, with shouts and imprecations, destitute even of the instinct which teaches a wild beast the way to its own den. Sounds of brawling, fighting, and revelry came from many of the rooms. Here a drunkard was kicking through the panels of a neighbour's door; there two dead-drunk women lay on a heap of straw; here a half-tipsy virago protested to us, with the air of a tragedy queen, that she "took in none but respectable lodgers;" there a man mad with drink tore his wife's throat with his nails. One room presented a scene of disgusting revelry and vice. In the next a feeble woman was stilling the moans of a dying child. "And that day was the preparation." It was the Edinburgh Saturday night, and over the din and discord of city sins, and over the wail of city sorrows, came the sweet sound of St. Giles's bells announcing that the Sabbath had begun.

Of that Saturday night in Edinburgh the Rev. R. Maguire, rector of Clerkenwell, who was one of our party, writes, in the Church of England Temperance Magazine--"We can but say that all we saw that night has left upon our mind the painful feeling, that of all the dark and desolate places of the earth the Old Town is about the darkest and the most desolate." He adds, in the same paper, after a description of some of the dwellings in Hume's Close--"We can scarcely feel surprised to know that the condition of these thousands is far past all hope."

Clerkenwell itself, Whitechapel, and Lambeth can furnish enough of misery and crime, but it is not believed that any city in Europe contains an area of wretchedness so large and unbroken as Edinburgh. In other cities the miserable dwellings and their inhabitants hide themselves out of sight in obscure purlieus, scarcely known to the rich by name, much less by observation. Here the very core of all is the High Street of the city, with a royal palace at one end and a royal castle at the other, and studded down the whole of its picturesque length with public buildings. Here are the Courts of Law, the Parliament House, the City Chambers, the Assembly Halls of the Established and Free Churches, the Cathedral, numerous places of worship, some of which at least are, or were, fashionable, newspaper offices, printing establishments, and one of the most frequented shops in the city, the wholesale and retail establishment of Duncan M'Laren and Son. Thus, instead of being hidden away, the wretchedness and vice of the High Street and Canongate obtrude themselves on all passers-by, from the representative of royalty who in semi-regal state passes up and down the whole extent of this Via Dolorosa, several times annually, to the summer swarm of tourists from all parts of the world, who return to their own cities rejoicing that they are not as the metropolis of Scotland. But it is not from such casual visitors that the amelioration of the condition of the poor is to be expected--not on them that the responsibility rests. It is on the gentlemen who cross the High Street daily to lounge in the Parliament House, on the literati who frequent one of the finest libraries in Britain, on the antiquarians who explore the wynds and closes in search of an ancient inscription or a remnant of a cornice, on the hundreds, both of ladies and gentlemen, whose avocations continually carry them to the various public offices in the High Street, on all who see and all who hear. Can it be that the feelings of all these are blunted by familiarity with sights which shock a stranger; or that the upper classes in Edinburgh are steeped in an unwholesome indifferentism; or that the Christianity of the city is waxing feeble and old? Without admitting one or all of these defects, it is difficult to account for the extreme complacency with which the majority of the upper classes are acting out the creed, "Forget the painful, suppress the disagreeable, banish the ugly;" content to add luxury to luxury, and to throw away money on ill-considered alms, while the poor are perishing from neglect. It is difficult to comprehend such intense apathy, after all that has been written by the daily press, private individuals, and lastly by the "Society for Improving the Condition of the Poor," to show the thinly-crusted abyss over which people are disporting themselves. It might have been supposed that when facts similar to those stated in these Notes have been reiterated from various quarters, so that no adult in Edinburgh can plead ignorance concerning the state of the poor, that the appeal for visitors made by the Society aforesaid would have met a tremendous and immediate response, and that the gentlemen of Edinburgh would have come forward, as those of other and busier cities have done, to offer willing aid. If there be another thing more mournful than the poverty and immorality of the poor, it is the vicious selfishness of the rich. It is observable in Edinburgh, as well as elsewhere, that the upper classes indulge very freely in the expression of opinion on the "dirt, vice, and improvidence of the poor," but the lapsed masses of the Old Town have a "public opinion" also regarding the selfishness, heartlessness, and indifference of the rich, and express it without much reticence of phraseology. Indeed, it is doubtful whether there is a man or woman who looks across the green ravine which separates the Old Town from the New, who has not a very decided opinion, right or wrong, that the negative and positive delinquencies of the best-instructed class have a great deal to do with the lapsing of the masses in this city. Almost the first steps have yet to be taken towards removing this baneful hostility of class, and promoting a healthy feeling on each side.

In "house-to-house visitation" in Edinburgh, I have observed with much surprise that among 145 families visited 143 were Scotch. In almost the whole of these the influence of a decent upbringing, and the restraints which connexion with a church imposes, had been thrown away, and the people, utterly debased and pauperized, had not a rag of Scottish pride left. It appears from all that can be observed that the mere existence of these unbroken masses of poverty, overcrowding, and vice, has a tendency to denationalize the people, and to produce a population which shall be absolutely barren of those virtues which have been considered peculiarly Scotch--a population, in fact, knowing nothing of truthfulness, modesty, reverence for parents and old age, independence, Sabbath observance, and thrift. These masses, which are sinking lower and lower, in spite of existing agencies, have little to distinguish them from the "dangerous classes" of London, Paris, or New York, except that they are more drunken and dirty. Their mere existence, to say nothing of their increase, is sapping the foundations of "Scottish nationality."

Another thing which impresses a stranger is a peculiar habit of speech common to nearly all these people, and is possibly nearly the only relic of their more religious days. "God-forgotten" was the phrase they nearly all used, an expression which gives occasion to the question, "Have Christians, who are the representatives of God upon earth, misrepresented Him to these people by their neglect?" A grudge against God, an idea as if He were the author of evil and not good to them, seemed general. Many of the phrases used showed a sort of reckless belief, which, under the circumstances, was worse than unbelief. Coming down a long dark stair late at night, from an overcrowded land, a frightful hag clutched my arm with her skinny hand, and hissed into my ear, "Is it God's elect you are seeking here? It's the devil's elect you'll find," laughing fiendishly at her own wit. "So this is Blackfriars Wynd," remarked one of our party, as we passed down the crowded alley. "No, it's hell's mouth," exclaimed a forlorn woman, who was dragging a drunken man to his joyless home. "Do you think the missionary would dare to mock me by telling me of God's love? Could he have the face to do it here?" a poor woman exclaimed, whose three fatherless children lay ill on some straw, which served for a bed in a cellar, of which it and a kettle were the only "furniture."

It is one thing to hear unpleasant facts stated by unwelcome speakers, or to meet with them fossilized in statistical tables, but altogether another to confront them in beings clothed in kindred flesh and blood, in men, women, and children claiming a common Fatherhood, and asserting their right to be heard. These our brethren, haggard, hopeless, hardened, vicious, on whose faces sin has graved deeper lines than either sorrow or poverty; this old age which is not venerable, this infancy which is not loveable, these childish faces, or faces which should have been childish, peering from amidst elvish locks, and telling of a precocious familiarity with sin,--these glowering upon us from the tottering West Bow, with its patched and dirty windows, from the still picturesque Lawnmarket, from the many-storeyed houses of the High Street,--these are spectres not easily to be laid to rest, and "polite society," which has become perfect in the polite art of indifference, must encounter them, sooner or later, in one way or another.

Surely it is possible to raise these our brethren, who are living and dying like brutes, to a platform on which the gospel of Him who came to preach glad tidings to the poor would not be met by nearly insuperable obstacles. Though more wretches have been pulled out of the mire by mission churches than by any other agency, the masses are "lapsed," "gone under," sunk on the whole to lower depths than the ministerial plummet can sound, and the ministers, most of whom are hampered by the existing necessities of large congregations, are not directly responsible for a condition of things which is a disgrace to Scottish Christianity. My own experience leads me to believe that these lapsed masses must be raised out of the "Slough of Despond" before they can hear or see; that these miserable thousands must have at least as much light, air, and space as we give our brutes, before a ministerial visit can be aught but a mockery,--before they can rise to manhood and womanhood in Christ. The ministers are not to be altogether blamed for failing to carry the tidings of peace to those who are too deaf, from drink and demoralization, to hear them. Condemn them if they fail to thunder into ears scarcely less dull, that the blood of those who are going down alive into the pit will be required of a church-membership which is bound to aim at no lesser measure of devotion than His who laid down His life for the brethren. Let them demand the lives of these godless ones from the respectable who enjoy the Sabbath luxury of sermons; let them declare a crusade against the Christlessness and apathy of those who sit at ease at communion-tables, content to leave those to the outer darkness for whom that same body and blood were broken and shed, and they will be guiltless.

It was by a life of sacrifice and a death of shame that the redemption of this world was wrought; and it is by a life of sacrifice alone--if loving search after the lost, if personal sympathy with the wretched, if stooping to raise and aid the poor are to be called sacrifice--that the Master's steps can be followed and His work on the earth be completed.

I. L. B.

FOOTNOTES

1. Report on the Condition of the Poorer Classes in Edinburgh, 1868, p. 19.

2. Report on the Condition of the Poorer Classes of Edinburgh, 1868, p. 49.

ABOUT ISABELLA LUCY BIRD

Early Life & Background

Isabella Lucy Bird entered the world in 1831 as the daughter of a prosperous Yorkshire family. Her childhood did not portend the adventurous life ahead. Instead, Bird suffered from persistent health issues that often left her confined indoors.

As a young girl, she endured debilitating headaches, spinal troubles, nervous disorders and other chronic ailments. While bedridden for long stretches, Isabella passed time and fed her imagination by immersing herself in books that brimmed with tales of travel and cultures beyond England's shores. With the limited mobility she experienced in her early years (due to nervous system disorders), reading was one of the most pleasant things she could do.

When in her early 20s, Isabella's desire for autonomy aligned providentially with her doctor's prescription to travel as a remedy. Having come from wealth, she now had the means to set sail as an unchaperoned woman gaining strength through adventure - a privilege that defied normal Victorian conventions.

Early Travels

In 1854 (at age 23) Isabella embarked on a monumental journey that launched her career as an explorer - setting sail for America and Canada on her first major solo trip. Funded by her family's wealth, Isabella spent nearly four months immersed in the frontier cultures of North America that had so enthralled during her years of convalescence.

This inaugural voyage nurtured the independence and resilience that defined Bird's adventurous spirit for the next fifty years. No longer confined to her bedroom in Yorkshire, the young woman who had dreamed of distant lands as an invalid now traversed sees and rugged landscapes as an explorer.

Two years later in 1856, Isabella traveled further west to pioneer Mormon settlements in Utah. During her time there, she honed the keen observational eye and literary acumen that allowed her to publish "The Englishwoman in America" - a memoir on transatlantic travels which cemented her fame as an intrepid female explorer and solidified her trailblazing status.

Though much of Isabella's early frailties had limited her mobility early in life, she now pushed forward with record-setting travels only previously accomplished by men.

Later Expeditions

Isabella spent the 1870s voyaging intrepidly across ever more remote corners of the world. From 1873-1875, she embarked on extensive travels exploring the depths of Asia, immersing herself in the vibrant diversity of Japan, China, Vietnam and beyond.

During her journeys across Eastern kingdoms, Isabella relied upon her fluency in language and culture to forge connections with inhabitants from all walks of life. Her vivid depictions of sights and encounters captured timeless insights even as global forces began to erode regional traditions.

When she yearned for further conquests, the Hawaiian archipelago and its towering volcanoes called to Bird's thirst for natural grandeur. Through the 1870s, she spent months traversing Hawaii's rugged wilderness terrain on solitary climbs many native guides dared not attempt. From snow-capped summits over 13,000 feet high, Isabella's pen poured forth lyrical admiration.

Her adventuresome spirit only grew with age. In her late 50s from 1889-1890, Bird traversed the Middle East through India's vibrant landscape, then to Kurdistan and Persia's arid mountain kingdoms - amassing still more tales for the Victorian audiences enraptured by her decades of boundary-shattering exploration.

Significant Achievements

Isabella's decades of intrepid global wanderlust cemented her legacy as a female explorer ahead of her time. In recognition of this, the Royal Geographical Society (in 1892) formally inducted her into their group of eminent explorers of her time.

Through over 10 acclaimed books published across her lifetime, Bird transported enraptured audiences on lyrical literary adventures spanning continents. Her prolific travelogues granted pioneering glimpses into remote cultures through a woman's eyes for readers back home.

But Bird's most enduring legacy remains the paths she blazed as a female lone explorer pushing limits across oceans and peaks at a time when prudence confined women close to home. Where prevailing wisdom cautioned that frail constitutions should shelter indoors, Isabella conquered 14,000 feet heights and roamed rugged wilderness for months sans companions at age 60 - living proof of what a determined women could endure.

With her courage and chronicles of the dizzying spaces she carved out for herself, Bird inspired future generations of female explorers and travelers to harbor ambitions beyond what society deemed possible. Though she passed in 1904 after seven decades of restless roaming, her intrepid spirit endures as a beacon to women – and men – with a desire for exploration.

ABOUT ISABELLA LUCY BIRD

Later Life & Death

In her late 50s, Isabella Bird opted to largely settle down in Edinburgh, Scotland - drawn by its thriving literary scene. Yet not even the comforts of home could still the wanderlust that had defined six decades of her life.

Though residing mainly in Edinburgh, Bird occasionally grew restless. When this happened, she once again embarked on another adventure. When not on the road, Bird's prolific pen sustained her as she published book after book recounting her decades of adventures for enraptured readers. Through her 60s and 70s, she produced a steady outpouring of memoirs and travelogues until her death.

To the end, the intrepid explorer stayed fiercely true to the enduring passions of her life – traveling the globe and enthralling audiences by pen as she tirelessly recorded her adventures. She departed the world in 1904 at the age of 72 as she had spent her life - immersed in literary travels still longing for the majestic beyond.

BOOKS BY ISABELLA LUCY BIRD

A Lady's Life in the Rocky Mountains: This book, written in 1879, is a collection of letters addressed to Bird's sister, documenting the incredible journeys of the explorer through the Colorado Rockies. Over six months, Bird traveled on horseback, covering more than 1,000 miles across largely uncharted wilderness. Each day posed uncertainty about where she would rest or spend the night. In her letters, Bird vividly describes the breathtaking beauty of the landscapes—snow-capped peaks, hidden valleys, and imposing canyons. However, the book's focal point lies in her poignant depictions of the enduring difficulties faced by the resilient pioneers she encountered. Bird witnessed firsthand the hardships of settlers making a living in the remote mountain settlements. She recounts scenes of isolated and basic cabins, lawlessness, the constant threat from Native tribes and outlaws, and the unforgiving harshness of winters with plummeting temperatures. Yet, amidst these challenges, Bird also admires the strength and integrity of the close-knit pioneer communities she visited. She forms meaningful connections during her weeks spent in isolated mining camps and ranches, assisting with cattle drives. Overall, this memoir serves as a vivid historical account of both culture and nature in the untouched Rocky Mountain frontier, offering a daring woman's perspective on this era.

Among the Tibetans: Published when Bird was 63 years old, this book recounts her challenging journeys across the high Tibetan Plateaus and the Himalayan mountain regions in the late 19th century. Starting her voyage in 1889, Bird explores lands like Ladakh, a region with a Tibetan culture bordering India. She crosses daunting mountain passes, some towering over 15,000 feet, entering Tibet proper and navigating to cities such as Lhasa and Gyantse. Bird is awestruck by the majestic peaks of the Great Himalayan Range, towering over high-altitude valleys and passes that test her physical endurance. She observes and documents cultures and Buddhist heritage largely unfamiliar to the Western world at that time. With her characteristic poetic style, Bird provides insights into the daily lives of remote Tibetan villages, largely untouched by modern influences. She develops a deep admiration for the principles and resourcefulness ingrained in their ancient traditions, enabling survival in a harsh, unforgiving landscape. As she journeys eastward on her return, Bird explores lesser-known Himalayan regions like Yarkand before heading back to India. Her memoir brought the mystique of enigmatic Tibet and Central Asia to Western audiences through the perspective of a pioneering female explorer traversing one of the world's most challenging terrains.

Chinese Pictures—Notes on Photographs Made in China: This book, first published in 1902, invites readers into the captivating world of China through the camera lens of one of history's most intrepid explorers. This compilation captures Isabella L. Bird's keen observations and vivid descriptions, complementing a series of photographs taken during her extensive travels across China. Through her lens and insightful prose, Bird unveils the essence of China's landscapes, people, and traditions. With each photograph, she weaves a narrative, providing a glimpse into the rich tapestry of Chinese life, from bustling cities to remote villages, picturesque landscapes to vibrant marketplaces. In her characteristic style, Bird delves into the cultural nuances, historical significance, and everyday moments frozen in time through the camera's lens. Her notes on the photographs offer a deeper understanding of the scenes captured, breathing life into the imagery and enhancing the reader's connection to the sights and stories behind each snapshot. 'Chinese Pictures' stands as a testament to Isabella L. Bird's ability to blend visual storytelling with her eloquent prose. This compilation serves as a captivating window into China's diverse landscapes and cultural heritage, painting a vivid portrait of the country through the lens of a pioneering traveler and perceptive observer."

Journeys in Persia and Kurdistan: This book, published when Bird was 59, recounts her bold and perilous travels through the regions of Persia (modern-day Iran) and Kurdistan in 1890. It provides a glimpse into a volatile period just before significant upheavals reshaped the fate of the region. Despite warnings about roaming bandits and tribal conflicts in the rural Ottoman and Persian frontiers, Bird was determined to venture into these areas, far from the usual tourist paths. Her Middle Eastern voyage took her through stunning yet unforgiving landscapes, where ancient ruins and bustling bazaars punctuated her journey. She relied on the hospitality of Kurdish and Persian village leaders while being guarded by armed escorts against desert marauders. With eloquent storytelling, Bird recounts her profound interactions with diverse regional cultures and religions, shedding light on the disdain towards oppressive Turkish rulers and offering glimpses into the practices of slavery and the harem system. Her engaging narrative provided Victorian readers with captivating insights into these distant lands, transporting them into the precarious realms at the fringes of crumbling empires on the verge of modernization sweeping through the Near East."

Korea and Her Neighbors: In this book, Bird chronicles her explorations through Korea and its surrounding regions during the late 19th century. Published at a time when knowledge about East Asian cultures was limited in the West, Bird's book provides an intimate portrayal of Korea and its relationships with neighboring countries. Embarking on her journey, Bird ventures into the heart of Korea, traversing its diverse landscapes and immersing herself in its unique traditions. She delves into the bustling streets of Seoul, experiencing the pulse of the country's dynamic capital. Throughout her travels, she embraces the local customs, witnessing the intricate cultural tapestry woven by the Korean people. Beyond the borders of Korea, Bird extends her exploration to the neighboring regions, unraveling the complex dynamics between Korea and its neighbors. She navigates through borderlands, encountering glimpses of life in China and Japan, and observes the interplay of cultures and influences at these junctions. Bird's vivid descriptions paint a captivating picture of Korea's rich heritage and the interactions between this enigmatic nation and its surrounding countries. Through her keen observations and engaging narrative, she provides readers with a nuanced understanding of the region, bridging the gap between the East and West during a transformative period in history.

Last Travels in West Africa: In this memoir, published just two years before Bird's passing at age 70, she recounts her final journeys to sub-Saharan Africa in the early 1900s, specifically focusing on British colonies like Sierra Leone and Nigeria. Starting in Freetown, Sierra Leone, Bird is captivated by the vibrant Creole communities thriving in trade after the collapse of the Atlantic slave routes. She immerses herself in exploring their bustling streets and also observes the customs of indigenous groups like the Timne people. Traveling by boat to Nigeria, Bird investigates cities such as Lagos and former slaving ports. Her journey takes her upriver to reach northern towns like Nupe. Throughout her travels, she meticulously documents the immense diversity of cultures, religions, livelihoods, and the sometimes controversial aspects of Britain's colonial rule. As an intrepid explorer defying societal expectations of retirement in old age, Bird ventures boldly across the region. Her memoir serves as an ethnographic study, shedding light on the complexity of British West Africa at the turn of the century, offering readers a deeper understanding beyond common stereotypes. Her vivid accounts in this memoir mark the culmination of a six-decade career exploring the world's farthest frontiers as a Victorian woman wanderer. Despite her age, she approached this adventure with the same courage and insight that characterized all her extraordinary exploits since her youth.

Notes on Old Edinburgh: In this book, Bird invites readers on a captivating journey through the historic streets and landmarks of Scotland's iconic capital. In this engaging work, Bird eloquently captures the essence of Old Edinburgh, transporting readers back in time to explore the city's rich history and vibrant character. With meticulous attention to detail, Bird traverses the cobblestone streets, unveiling the layers of history etched into the city's architecture, alleys, and renowned landmarks. Her keen observations breathe life into the nooks and crannies of Edinburgh, reviving the spirit of bygone eras. Through her vivid descriptions and insightful commentary, Bird sheds light on the city's storied past, delving into its medieval roots, royal connections, and cultural heritage. She navigates through the charming corners of Edinburgh, sharing tales of its inhabitants, traditions, and the enduring charm that has captivated visitors for centuries. 'Notes on Old Edinburgh' stands as a testament to Bird's knack for storytelling and historical preservation. Her evocative prose invites readers to stroll alongside her through the winding streets of this ancient city, painting a captivating portrait of Edinburgh's captivating allure and its timeless significance in Scottish history.

Six Months in the Sandwich Islands: In this classic work, published the same year as Bird's renowned 'The Hawaiian Archipelago,' she compiles letters she wrote to her sister Henrietta during her extensive six-month exploration of the Hawaiian Islands in 1873. This work provides a detailed account of her diverse adventures across Hawaii's eight major islands. Starting from Honolulu, Bird explores the volcanic slopes of Maui and Hawaii, the lush valleys of Kauai, and the coral-fringed atoll of Molokai. Throughout her journey, Bird revels in the lush tropical abundance of the islands, vividly capturing the ever-changing landscape shaped by volcanoes and the ocean. She immerses herself in the vibrant indigenous culture of the Native Hawaiians, documenting their traditions, artifacts, folklore, and more. However, the most captivating parts of her narrative recount Bird's daring escapades into Hawaii's rugged wilderness—solo climbs that even native guides hesitated to attempt. She delights in crossing treacherous rivers, ascending steep ravines, and camping in remote forests amidst wild storms. These experiences test her physical limits while fueling her adventurous spirit. Through her letters, readers witness Bird's transformation from an ailing Victorian woman to a fearless horsewoman and mountaineer. Her engaging writing style transports readers into the heart of ancient Hawaii's untamed landscapes and traditional ways of life.

The Aspects of Religion in the United States of America: Published merely three years after her initial American memoir, 'The Aspects of Religion in the United States of America' dives into the religious tapestry Isabella Bird encountered during her travels in the US. It provides an extensive exploration of the major Christian denominations she encountered, shedding light on lesser-known sects and emerging faith groups. From the lively camp meetings of Methodists to the simplicity of Quaker practices and the closely-knit Mormon communities out west, Bird covers a diverse array of religious experiences in this captivating book. She actively participates in and keenly observes various religious services, dissecting doctrines, rituals, clothing, and the architectural spaces tied to different churches. Beyond formal religious practices, the book delves into broader dimensions, such as the pervasive influence of Christian morality on American laws and social norms during the country's formative years. Bird also highlights how churches championed social causes, from temperance movements to anti-slavery activism. This book serves as an anthropological exploration of Christianity's role in everyday 19th-century America through Bird's perceptive lens. It offered unprecedented insights for British readers of her time and continues to captivate modern audiences with its depth and relevance."

The Englishwoman in America: Written in 1856, 'The Englishwoman in America' is Isabella Bird's memoir chronicling her inaugural overseas journey to the United States and Canada at 23 years old. Lasting nearly four months, her expedition covered vast stretches of the eastern U.S. and Canada. Health improvement motivated Bird, spurred by doctors who believed travel could be therapeutic. Departing from Britain, she landed in Halifax, Nova Scotia, then ventured southward to New York, Philadelphia, and Washington D.C. Her observations, as an outsider, offer keen insights into life in America's emerging frontier towns and cities. Bird paints a vivid picture of cultural nuances—social customs, politics, material culture, and architectural landscapes. She also draws comparisons between American and British ways. Amidst her social commentary, Bird beautifully captures the raw beauty of American wilderness, showcasing landscapes like the Catskill Mountains and Niagara Falls. This initial book, launching over four decades of bold travels and subsequent publications, foretold Isabella's future renown as an explorer and captivating writer. Her travelogues became sought-after windows into distant lands, presented uniquely through a woman's perspective for Victorian audiences."

The Golden Chersonese and the Way Thither: In this book, Bird transports readers on a mesmerizing journey through the exotic and mysterious landscapes of the Malay Peninsula. Written with the allure of an explorer's journal, this book recounts Bird's intrepid travels through the vibrant and enigmatic region. Setting out on her exploration, Bird takes readers along ancient trade routes and uncharted paths, immersing herself in the diverse cultures and breathtaking landscapes of the Malay Peninsula. From bustling ports to remote villages, she captures the essence of the people and places she encounters. Bird's narrative unfolds as a vivid tapestry of the peninsula's history, traditions, and natural wonders. She explores the lush jungles, encountering fascinating flora and fauna, and navigates through the dynamic tapestry of Malay society, observing the customs and rituals that shape its identity. Throughout her journey, Bird's keen observations and evocative prose offer readers a glimpse into the region's rich past and its present-day allure. 'The Golden Chersonese and the Way Thither' serves as an invaluable window into the captivating allure of the Malay Peninsula, weaving together history, adventure, and cultural immersion in a way that captivates the imagination.

The Hawaiian Archipelago: In this 1875 travel memoir, Isabella Bird recounts her captivating journey through the enchanting Hawaiian Islands in 1873 at the age of 41. The narrative focuses on her daring exploration, particularly her challenging treks up two of the world's tallest volcanoes located on the Big Island: Mauna Loa and Mauna Kea. Starting her journey on Oahu, Bird explores the bustling city of Honolulu and the verdant windward valleys before setting sail for Hawaii's Big Island. There, she is mesmerized by the ever-changing volcanic landscapes shaped by the continuous eruptions of Mauna Loa and Kilauea over the years. Driven by a quest for adventure, Bird embarks on a courageous 13-hour ascent of Mauna Kea, scaling its 14,000-foot icy summit without guides. The solitude and breathtaking views fuel her spirit. Buoyed by this accomplishment, she ventures to conquer Mauna Loa, the largest volcano on Earth. Camping along the way, she reaches the summit ridge at nearly 13,700 feet, gazing over the vast crater Mokuaweoweo. Bird's journey is marked by overcoming steep trails, high altitudes, freezing nights without proper shelter, and physical exhaustion—defying societal expectations for a supposedly delicate Victorian woman. Her poetic descriptions of Hawaii's volcanoes helped introduce their magnificence to the Western world. The allure of the landscape deeply captivated Bird, drawing her back to the islands in later years whenever she yearned for tropical adventures.

The Yangtze Valley and Beyond: Published when Bird was 68, this book recounts her extensive travels through China, Japan, and Korea during the 1890s. The highlight of her journey involves navigating the Yangtze River Valley aboard a houseboat. This later addition to Bird's collection primarily focuses on her exploration of China, covering both its inland regions and eastern coastline. Traveling along the Yangtze River, Asia's longest river, Bird observes vibrant river commerce that predates Western trade by centuries. She delves into cities like Nanjing and Wuhan, shedding light on China's interior, going beyond the well-known Treaty Ports. Over the following years, Bird ventures northward, exploring Beijing to witness remnants of Imperial dynasties and iconic sites such as the Great Wall. Continuing her offbeat path, she travels through Manchuria by rail to Harbin, witnessing the enduring impacts of Russian imperialism on the northern frontiers. Crossing the Yellow Sea by ship, Bird extends her voyage through Korea and Japan, observing the significant modernization reshaping East Asian nations at the turn of the 20th century. She passes through places like Port Arthur before returning to Scotland, where she compiled her detailed notes into a memoir for eager readers.

Unbeaten Tracks in Japan: This book chronicles Bird's 1878 journey through Japan, focusing on its remote northern and central areas seldom explored by foreigners. She adopts an unconventional writing style, offering a unique narrative of her off-the-beaten-path adventures. Rather than sticking to the bustling cities, Bird ventures deep into Japan's countryside and less-traveled regions. She discovers feudal villages largely untouched by Western influence, witnessing a fascinating blend of ancient customs and the modernization of the Meiji era. A highlight of her expedition is her trek to Hokkaido, Japan's northernmost main island, where she encounters the indigenous Ainu people. She's captivated by their culture while noting the encroaching imperialist influences threatening their traditional way of life. Throughout her travels, Bird vividly portrays picturesque landscapes—mountains, lakes, and rural scenes populated by farmers and artisans harmonizing with nature. With a mix of literary references, historical insights, and poetic language, Bird weaves an eccentric travel saga that mirrors the mystical realm she explored. 'Unbeaten Tracks in Japan' presented the charms of old Japanese culture to Western readers through a distinctive feminine perspective."

www.ingramcontent.com/pod-product-compliance
Lightning Source LLC
Chambersburg PA
CBHW050045080526
44586CB00014B/1472